Micı

CU00982555

Woodbridge Walks

15 Circular Walks in and around Woodbridge

Geoff Gostling

ISBN 0-9525478-5-6

Printed by Portman Press
Published by G J Gostling
Copyright © G J Gostling

Cover Picture: Evening at Woodbridge Tide Mill

CONTENTS

Foreword   3

Introduction   4

About the Area   4

Walks

* Please note that walks 1, 2, 3, 4 and 15 also appear in the revised (1996) edition of West Deben Walks.

Foreword

Micro Ramblers are local walk books. Each book in the series contains 15 walks in a comparatively small area. These are almost always circular, and often linked so that two or more may be joined to form longer walks if required.

Instructions for each individual walk are contained on the right-hand page, with the relevant map on the left, so there's no need to turn over pages while you're walking (unless you're joining 2 or more together).

The average length of walks in this book is 6km (4 miles). The scale of sketch maps is 4cm to 1km or 2½in to 1 mile. (but not the overall map on page 36)

All walks use rights of way*, permissive paths or unclassified roads. Limited use is made of main roads for joining paths or getting to and from car parks.

Distances are given in metres and kilometres. If you're more at home with yards and miles, it may be of help to remember that 1 yard is about 1 metre, 800 metres is a half-mile, 1½km is about 1 mile.

Times are based on average walking speeds. As a rough guide, at an average walking speed, it takes about 12 minutes to walk 1km, or just over 1 minute to walk 100m.

Country Walking

Right of Way means that you have a right of passage over the ground, but no right to stray from the path. You also have a right to expect that paths be unobstructed. Clearly farmers have to work the land, but footpaths should be rolled within 2 weeks of ploughing, if weather permits.

Please remember the Country Code. Machinery, livestock and crops are the farmers livelihood. Help them, and help preserve wildlife by observing a few simple rules:

Guard against risk of fire;	Take litter home
Protect wildlife plants & trees;	Use gates & stiles to cross fences;
Fasten gates;	Leave livestock alone;
Keep pets under control;	Don't pollute water;
Keep to rights of way;	Don't make unnecessary noise;

Introduction

'Woodbridge Walks' is the 6th in the Micro Rambler Series, and contains 15 circular walks within 5 miles (8km) of Woodbridge.

Some of the walks are duplicated in West Deben Walks, which covers the bank of the Deben from Felixstowe Ferry to Ufford. The duplicated walks are numbers 1, 2, 3, 4 and 15.

There is a signposted trail from Woodbridge to Witnesham called the Fynn Valley Path. Several of the walks in the book take in elements of this. Taken in sequence, walks 2, 1, 15, 13 and 12 will give you a sense of continuity along much of the Fynn Valley.

Walking in Suffolk

Signposting of footpaths and bridleways in Suffolk has improved considerably in the last few years. Yellow arrows are often found on field edges to help you find your way. This sometimes occurs when a path has been re-routed. If instructions in the book seem to differ from these, it may mean the path has been re-routed since the book was last revised. In this case please observe any obvious indications of a new route.

About the Area

Bealings (Great and Little) Two pleasant villages between Woodbridge and Ipswich. There is only one pub - The Admiral's Head near Little Bealings church. (Walks 11 and 13).

Bredfield and Boulge Bredfield is another pleasant village with a good pub, the Castle. Boulge is shown as a parish on the local map but is hard to identify as a 'place', unless one chooses Boulge church, the burial place of the poet, Edward Fitzgerald. There is a footpath from the back of Bredfield church across the fields taking you directly towards Boulge church. (Walk 9 takes you for part of the way)

Bromeswell This small village is so quiet that you may walk all the way along Common Lane and not see a car. It is the only place in this book that's on the east side of the river Deben. Unfortunately there's no pub but there's a pretty little 15th century church.

Grundisburgh   A most attractive village with a handsome church. There's a good village pub, The Dog, a village green with a stream running through it and a ford.

Martlesham Once a well known village to travellers on the A12, but now mercifully bypassed. There are 2 pubs, The Black Tiles, a fairly modern roadhouse, and the Red Lion, which is also a carvery

Melton Since it is difficult to 'see the join', you could be forgiven for thinking that Melton is a suburb of Woodbridge. There are 2 churches in Melton, a new one visible on Walk 3, and Melton Old Church, passed by Walk 4. There are 2 pubs in Melton, but neither of them on any of the walks in the book.

Pettistree.   An attractive little village just outside Wickham Market. There's a pleasant little pub, the Greyhound, next to an interesting church.

Playford Playford church stands high on a steep bank above the road and is well worth a visit. Playford Hall is a splendid building seen on Walk 12. Unfortunately there's no pub in the village, but 2 of the walks starting here go past the Admiral's Head in Little Bealings.

Ufford   Ufford is an attractive village, known mainly for the church. This has one of the most ornately carved and largest font covers in East Anglia, reaching nearly to the roof.   The most attractive parts of the village are those away from the B1438, down towards the freshwater Deben. There are 2 pubs, The Crown, on the B1438, and the (White) Lion near the river.

Wickham Market   It's several hundred years since Wickham Market actually had a market but it is still worth a visit.   There's an attractive church with an octagonal tower. The nearest pub to the walks is the White Hart in the square.

Woodbridge   One of the most attractive towns in Suffolk with places of interest too numerous to mention. Some of the better known are The Tide Mill, the Seckford Almshouses, the Shire Hall, the Steelyard and Buttrums Mill. The picturesque quayside must be seen. Wander round the old streets - you'll find plenty to please the eye.

Map 1

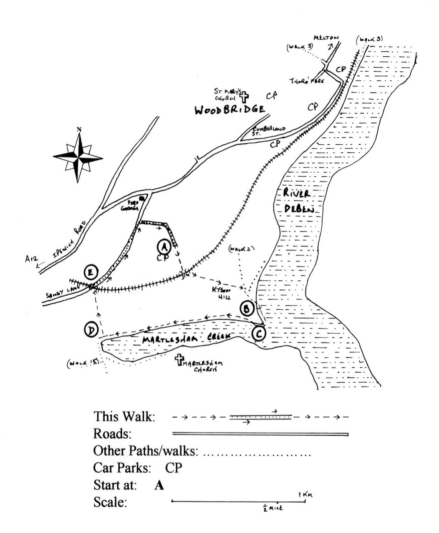

This Walk:	- → - - → - ══════⋯⋯⋯ - → - - → -
Roads:	══════════
Other Paths/walks:	………………………
Car Parks:	CP
Start at:	**A**
Scale:	

Walk 1

Distance: 3km (2m) 1 hour approx.
Start Point: Kyson Hill Car Park (GR 264478)
Route: Kyson Hill, Martlesham Creek
Pubs: None on route, but plenty in Woodbridge
Car Parking: 400m (1/4 mile) down Broomheath, off Sandy Lane

A: Leave the car park, go out onto the lane and turn right towards the river, soon crossing the bridge over the railway. Note the fine views from the top of Kyson Hill after this.

B: At the point where the river promenade joins from the left, turn right, soon descending onto the beach at Kyson Point. (If the tide is in, the shore could be covered, and you may have to wait for some time - the only right of way is along the shore.)

C: At Kyson Point turn right along the rail fence, to reach Martlesham Creek river wall in about 150m. Go onto the wall and walk along to the head of the creek.

D: When you reach the T-junction at the head of the creek, turn right. In about 300m, you'll reach a narrow metalled road. (Sandy Lane).

E: Turn right along Sandy Lane, and in about 600m turn right again into Broomheath to return to the car park.

Map 2

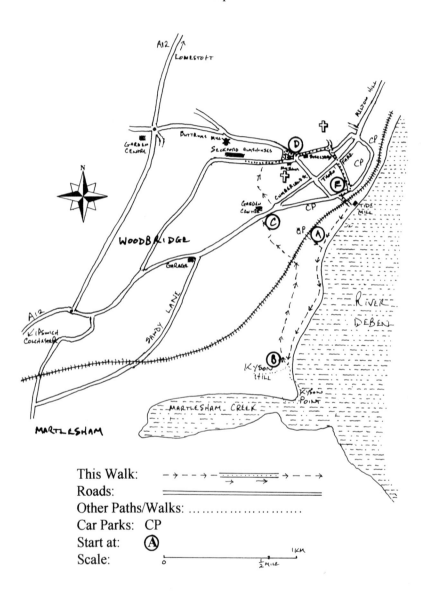

This Walk: $- \rightarrow - - \rightarrow -$ $\cdots\cdots$ $\rightarrow - - \rightarrow$

Roads:

Other Paths/Walks: ....

Car Parks: CP

Start at: Ⓐ

Scale:

Walk 2

Distance: 5km (3m) 1-1½ hours
Start Point: Woodbridge Promenade (GR 273485)
Route: Kyson Hill, Shire Hall, Steelyard, Tide Mill
Pubs: Various
Car Park: Small car park at bottom of Kingston Road

A: Leave the car park, cross the railway line, and turn right along the river wall. Stay on this to reach the National Trust sign at the bottom of Kyson Hill.

B: At the N.T. sign turn right on the signed track along the bottom of Kyson Hill. Stay on this pleasant track to reach a level crossing in about 600m. After crossing the railway, go straight up the track on the other side. At the top turn right on the road for about 50m, then take the first road on the left (Cherry Tree Road). At the top you'll reach the Ipswich Road near Notcutts garden centre.

C: Turn right, passing the garden centre, then, shortly afterwards, turn left into Fen Walk. Go straight along Fen Walk to emerge in Fen Meadow in about 250m. Turn right along the fence to reach Seckford Street. *If you want to have a look at the Seckford Almshouses turn left on Seckford Street, and walk along for about 250m, before returning to this point.* Turn right on Seckford Street to reach Market Hill in about 250m. *Note the Shire Hall with the Horse Museum above. The Town Museum is in the terrace on your right, and St Mary's church is behind the terrace.*

D: Having entered Market Hill at the top right hand corner, leave it at the bottom left hand corner via New Street, soon passing under the old Steelyard. At the bottom of the hill, go past the library and car park to reach the Thoroughfare, the main shopping street.

E: Go straight across the Thoroughfare into the narrow road opposite and continue down to the main road at the bottom. Here turn right and walk along to Tide Mill Way on the left in about 100m. Turn into Tide Mill Way, and walk down almost as far as the Tide Mill, before turning right along the promenade. Stay on the river wall now to return to your start point.

Map 3

This Walk: → – – → – – ⇉ → – – → –
Roads: ══════════════
Other Paths/walks: ....
Car Parks: CP
Start at: (A)
Scale:

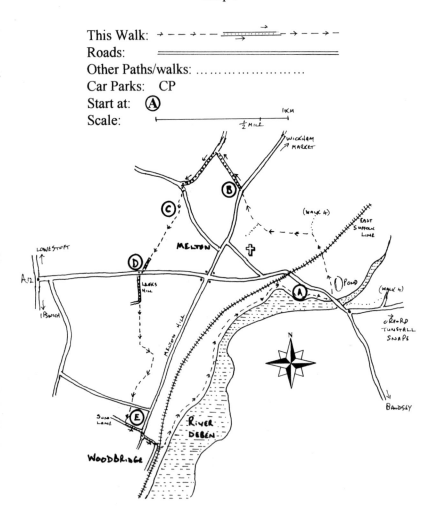

1KM
½ MILE

WICKHAM
MARKET

(B)

(WALK 4)

EAST
SUFFOLK
LINE

(C)

LOWESTOFT

MELTON

A12

(D)

POND

(WALK 4)

(A)

IPSWICH

LARKS
HILL

ORFORD
TUNSTALL
SNAPE

MELTON HILL

N

BAWDSEY

SUN
LANE

(E)

RIVER
DEBEN

WOODBRIDGE

Walk 3

Distance: 7½ km (4½m) 1½ - 2 hours.
Start Point: Melton Riverside Picnic Site (GR288503)
Route: Melton, Woodbridge, River bank path.
Pubs: Wilford Bridge at Melton, various pubs at Woodbridge
Car Parking: Melton Picnic Site and Car Park (Height Barrier 2.3m)

A: From the car park, cross the small wooden bridge to reach the river wall. Turn left on the wall and walk along to the road bridge. Cross the road and go along the metalled lane opposite. After crossing the railway, keep straight on for about 200m, then follow the path round to the left. Stay on the main path to reach the Ufford/Melton road.

B: Go straight across onto the narrow road opposite. In about 400m, turn left at the T-junction. In another 400m, immediately after a right hand bend, you'll reach another T-junction. Turn left again and in about 50m, turn right onto a signed path. The track soon enters a field.

C: Cross to the field edge on the left, and follow it along for about 200m to the corner. Here go through a gap and walk downhill on an ill-defined, often muddy path. At the bottom, cross a stile, a plank bridge and another stile to enter a paddock. Go very slightly right to a stile almost opposite (next to a small shed). After crossing the stile, turn left into the lane, then left into a side road to reach a main road.

D: Turn right on the main road for a short distance, then turn left up Leeks Hill. In 200m go straight on where the private road bends right. Keep straight on for about 350m to reach a signposted T-junction. Here turn left downhill bringing you out in a lane. Turn right in the lane and follow it to pass a new housing estate on the right. Immediately after this, turn right along a shady lane to reach a road in about 300m . Cross into the lane opposite and walk along to reach another road (Sun Lane).

E: Turn left in Sun Lane, and walk along to the main road. Turn right for a few steps, then turn left at the traffic lights onto Lime Kiln Quay Road. On the next right hand bend, cross the level crossing and turn immediately left on a narrow path, soon taking you to the river wall. Follow this along for about 2km to reach the picnic site car park over to your left.

Map 4

This Walk: →- -→ - ⟹ →- -→ -
Roads: ═══════
Other Paths/Walks: ....
Car Parks: CP
Start At: Ⓐ
Scale: |0̶————————1 KM̶ |
         ½ MILE

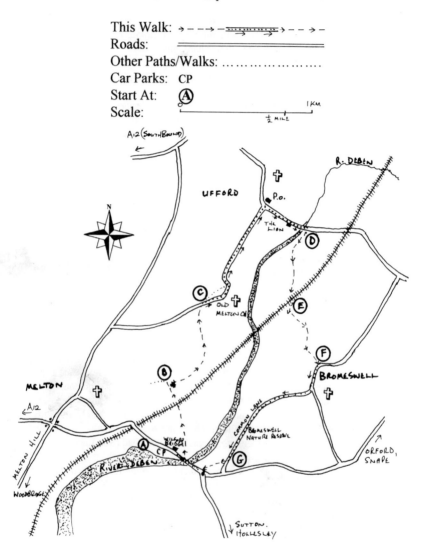

Walk 4

Distance: 6½ km (4m) 1½ hours approx
Start Point: Melton Picnic Site (GR288503)
Route: Ufford, Bromeswell, Bromeswell Nature Reserve
Pubs: The Wilford Bridge at Melton and The Lion at Ufford
Car Parking: Melton Picnic Site and Car Park (Height Barrier 2.3m)

***If the tide's out,, you may be able to take the short cut back to Wilford
Bridge at 'G' below. Otherwise you'll have to stay on the road***

A: Go to the river wall and turn left. At the bridge, cross the road and go
down the lane opposite. Cross the railway and go straight on for 200m.

B: Where the track bends left, go through a gap on the right behind a
triple garage. Follow this clear field edge path, soon becoming a farm
track, to reach a road at a T-junction in 700m.

C: Turn right on the road, and stay on it to reach Ufford, passing Melton
Old Church on the way. At Ufford post office at the T-junction, turn
right, passing the Lion pub. In 200m you'll reach 2 bridges.

D: After the first bridge, turn right on a clear path, crossing a footbridge
almost immediately. After crossing a stile in about 150m, follow the river
round to the right for a few steps, then turn left along the field edge. Stay
on this path with the stream on your left to reach a river and rail crossing.

E: Cross the stream and railway and turn right. The path angles slightly
away from the ditch to a footbridge in a line of willows. After crossing the
bridge, turn left for about 200m to reach a track. Turn right on the track,
and stay on it to reach the road in Bromeswell.

F: At the road turn right, and at the junction in 150m keep right in
Common Lane. Stay on this almost all the way to the main road in 1km.

G: 75m before the main road, if the tide's low, you can turn right on a
footpath through reeds to Wilford Bridge. *This can be muddy even at low
tide, since it is frequently covered.* If in doubt, stay on the road to the top,
turn right, then right again to bring you back to the bridge.

Map 5

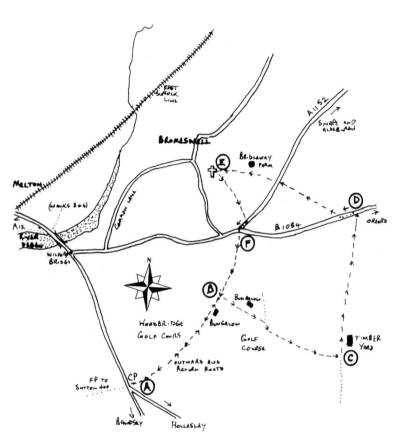

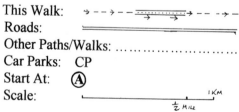

This Walk: ⇢ – – ⇢ – – ⇢ ⋯⋯⋯→ → ⇢ – – ⇢ – –

Roads: ══════════════

Other Paths/Walks: ⋯⋯⋯⋯⋯⋯⋯⋯⋯⋯

Car Parks: CP

Start At: Ⓐ

Scale: |——————————| 1 KM
             ½ MILE

- 14 -

Walk 5

Distance: 7km (4½m) 1½-2 hours
Start Point: Sutton Hoo Car Park (GR 297491)
Route: Woodbridge Golf Course, Bromeswell Church
Pub: Not on direct route (Nearest is the Cherry Tree, Bromeswell)
Car Parking: See Start Point

A: Leave from the rear right hand side of the car park on the wide signed track. In about 50m, at the clearing, follow the track round to the left, and in another 50m go through the gate and continue along the edge of the golf course, with the fence on your right. In 600m, where the fence bends right, follow the direction of the FP sign slightly left. In 100m you'll pass a small bungalow on the right.

B: 100m after the bungalow, turn right on a signed path. Keep along the left hand edge of the golf course, eventually entering a track alongside a line of pines. Go through the small gate straight ahead at the end, then turn right along the fence. In about 50m turn left onto a good track and stay on it for about 600m to reach a T-junction.

C: At the T-junction, turn left, immediately passing a timber yard. Stay on this wide track, keeping more or less straight ahead to reach a road in about 1200m.

D: Turn left on the road (B1084) for about 100m, then turn down a signed track to the right. Stay on this for about 600m to reach the A1152. Go straight across onto the track opposite, signed 'Bridleway Farm' for about 500m to reach Bromeswell church.

E: Just before reaching the church turn left on a signed path and stay on it to reach the A1152 near the junction with the B1084. Walk down to the junction.

F: Immediately opposite the junction, take the wide track uphill alongside the plantation. In about 500m, where the track bends left, go through a gate onto the golf course, and follow signs taking you back past the small bungalow, then onwards up the side of the golf course to return to the car park.

Map 6

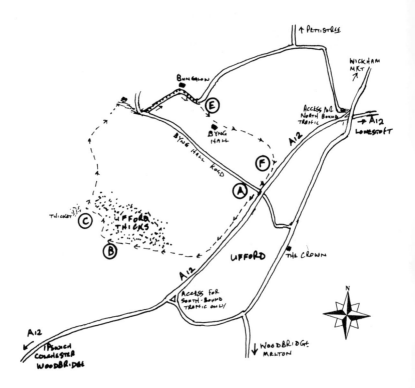

This Walk: →－→－→ ⊦⊦⊦⊦⊦⊦⊦⊦⊦⊦⊦＞－－→－→
Roads: ═══════════
Other Paths/walks: ....
Car Parks: CP
Start at: (A)
Scale:

Walk 6

Distance: 5km (3m) 1 hour approx
Start Point: Byng Hall Road, Ufford (GR 292534)
Route: Ufford Thicks and Byng Hall
Car Parking: Roadside parking on Byng Hall Road*
Pubs: The Crown, Ufford (near entrance to Byng Hall Road)

Park on verge just after passing under the A12

A: Go back towards the bridge, and turn right along the well-surfaced track parallel with the A12. In about 700m stay on the track as it swings right away from the road. In about another 250m you'll enter a wood (Ufford Thicks). Keep on along the track on the inside left-hand edge of the wood, ignoring the left turn into a conifer plantation. In about 400m you'll reach an open field.

B: At the open field, keep on along the edge of the wood as it swings right then left again.

C: Follow the main wood round, passing a small thicket separate from the wood. About 150m after the thicket, at the next corner of the wood, keep straight on along the field edge path for about 500m to reach a farm track.

D: Turn right on the track, passing a house called Silver Birches, then some farm buildings. When you reach the road on a bend, keep right, and in a further 50m turn left on a side road. After passing a pink bungalow on a right-hand bend, stay on the road for about 200m to reach a left-hand bend.

E: Where the road bends left, go straight on along a signed field edge path. After crossing a stile by some buildings (Byng Hall), keep on with the buildings on your right to reach a farm road. After a few steps the road swings right and here keep straight on with the field edge on your right. Stay alongside the field edge all the way to the A12.

F: At the A12, turn right and follow the post and rail fence along the bottom of the embankment, to reach the road at your start point.

Map 7

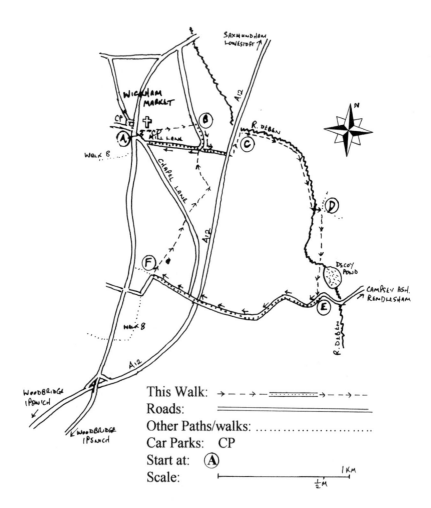

This Walk: →--→ — ...... →--→--

Roads: =====

Other Paths/walks: ....

Car Parks: CP

Start at: (A)

Scale: |————————| 1 KM

½ M

- 18 -

Walk 7

Distance: 7km (4½m) 1½ hours approx
Start Point: Wickham Market (GR303557)
Route: River Deben and Wickham Market
Car Parking: Car Park in Chapel Street next to Medical Centre

A: Leave the car park by the path alongside the medical centre, and enter the churchyard. Turn right and walk down the tree-lined lane. When you reach the terrace turn left into a lane, following it round to the right shortly afterwards. After passing through a kissing gate and down the edge of the field, go straight on across an open field to reach a road. (Spring Lane)

B: Turn right in Spring Lane for about 300m, then turn left to pass under the A12. Immediately after passing under the main road, turn left and walk along to reach the River Deben in about 300m.

C: Turn right along the bank of the Deben, and follow the river closely for about 1½km to cross 2 footbridges, the second taking you across the main river. After crossing the Deben walk on for about 50m to reach a 4-way footpath sign.

D: Turn right at the footpath sign to follow a field edge path. Keep along the field edge to reach the river Deben again in about 400m. Cross the concrete bridge and continue along the track on the other side to reach a road in about another 300m.

E: Turn right on this meandering road, and follow it for about 1½km to cross the A12 again. After crossing the main road, continue on for about another 300m to where the road bends sharp left.

F: On the left-hand bend, turn right on a signed track. Follow this for about 600m to reach a narrow road (Chapel Lane). Cross Chapel Lane, and continue on the green track opposite. In about 800m, when you reach Mill Lane in Wickham Market, turn left and walk up the lane for about 600m to return to the car park.

Map 8

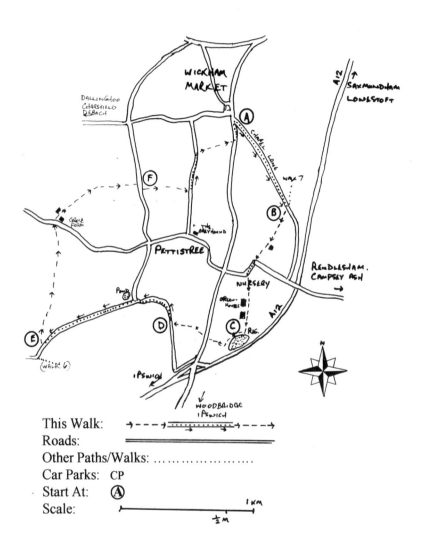

This Walk: → – – → ∙∙∙∙∙∙∙∙∙ → – – →
Roads: ══════════
Other Paths/Walks: ....
Car Parks: CP
Start At: Ⓐ
Scale: |————————————| 1 KM
                ½ M

Walk 8

Distance: 7km (4½m) 1½-2 hours
Start Point: Wickham Market (GR303557)
Route: Wickham Market, Pettistree
Car Parking: Chapel Lane Car Park

A: Go out into Chapel Lane and turn left. Stay in Chapel Lane for about 600m to reach signed footpaths to right and left.

B: Turn right on the grassy track and keep straight on to reach a road at a bend in about 500m. Go straight on at the road, and where the road bends right take the signed path on a concrete road through the nursery. 100m after passing a large greenhouse on the right, cross a stile and turn right alongside a reservoir.

C: Follow the path round, soon reaching a sign taking you to the right through the plantation. After crossing a stile, turn right on the track to reach the main road. Go straight across the road on the signed path opposite and follow it to reach another road in about 400m. (*If this path is too overgrown, turn left at the main road then turn right on a narrow side road - this soon bends right, bringing you to the other end of this path in about 800m*)

D: Turn right on this narrow road, soon following it round to the left to reach a pond in about 400m. Here turn left at the side road signed Hungarian Hall. Stay on this road, ignoring the cul-de-sac in about 150m. 600m after the cul-de-sac, immediately after passing downhill under the power lines, you'll reach a signed track on the right.

E: Turn right on this pleasant track and stay on it to reach a road by Grove Farm in about 1km. Cross the road and continue straight on along the signed path between farm buildings. After passing the buildings the farm road enters a long field. Keep more or less to the centre of the field, aiming for the far corner. Go through the gate in the corner and continue along the track to reach a road in about 300m.

F: At the road, go briefly right then left on a signed path. Follow this field edge path for about 400m to reach a road. Turn left on the road for about 350m, then turn right on a field edge path. When you reach the road in 300m, turn left to return to the Chapel Lane car park.

Map 9

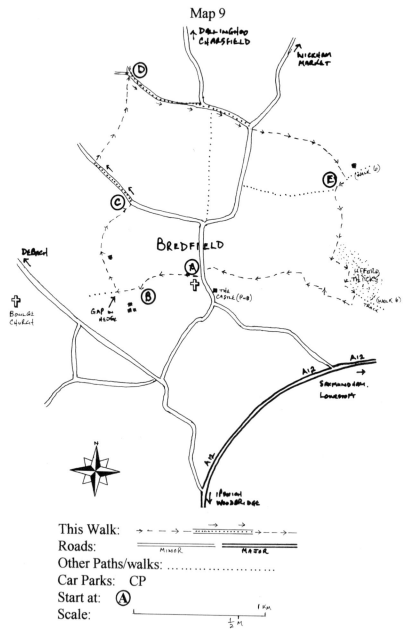

This Walk: →←——→——⋯⋯⋯⋯→——→—
Roads: ═══════ MINOR   ══════ MAJOR
Other Paths/walks: ⋯⋯⋯⋯⋯⋯⋯⋯⋯
Car Parks: CP
Start at: Ⓐ
Scale: |————————| 1 KM
        ½ M

- 22 -

Walk 9

Distance: 8km (5m) 1½ - 2 hours.
Start Point: Bredfield near the church (GR269530)
Route: Bredfield circular
Pubs: The Castle
Car Parking: Roadside Parking near the church

A: Go through to the back of the churchyard. *Note the group of red-roofed farm buildings half left with a gap in the hedge 50m right of these* Go through the kissing gate and then straight on between the two fields. In about 250m the right of way goes slightly left to reach a field edge. Follow this field edge taking you roughly towards the buildings mentioned above.

B: A short distance along the field edge towards the buildings you should find a path across the field to the gap mentioned above. (*If the path isn't clear, stay on the field edge until it bends left, then head straight for the gap in the hedge*) At the gap, turn right along the hedge towards a house with unusual chimneys. Follow the path past the pond in front of the house to reach a surfaced track on the other side. Stay on the track to reach the corner of a road.

C: At the corner, turn left to pass under power lines in about 200m. About 200m after the power lines turn right on a signed path alongside a wood. At the far end of the field, go through the wood briefly, then out onto the field edge again in the same direction, to reach a road in 400m.

D: Turn right on the narrow road. At the junction in 600m keep straight on. Where the road bends right in another 500m, by a pond, continue straight on across the field on a signed path. Cross a ditch by a wide wooden bridge and continue up the field in the same direction. At the next field edge, your route changes slightly taking you about 50m right of a cream coloured house. Cross the ditch via a plank bridge and turn right on a track for about 100m to reach a footpath sign.

E: Turn left at the sign, and follow the field edge path to reach a wood (Ufford Thicks). Keep on along the edge of the wood, following it left, right then left again until the path becomes a wider track. Don't enter the track, but turn right along the field edge for about 100m, then right again towards Bredfield. Keep along field edge and ditch to reach the village.

Map 10

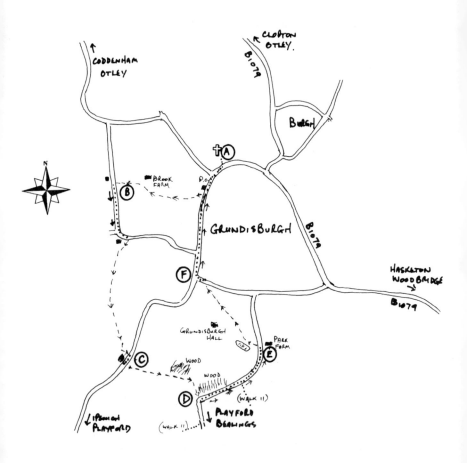

This Walk: → — → — ⁚⁚⁚⁚⁚⁚⁚⁚⁚⁚⁚⁚⁚ — → — — →

Roads: ════════════

Other Paths/walks: ....

Car Parks: CP

Start at: Ⓐ

Scale: |————————————| 1 Km
                    ½ M

- 24 -

Walk 10

Distance: 5½km (3½m) 1 - 1½ hours.
Start Point: Grundisburgh Village Green near church (GR224511)
Route: Grundisburgh circular
Pubs: The Dog
Car Parking: See Start Point

A: From the church, cross to the main road and turn right. (signed Tuddenham, Ipswich and Culpho). A few steps after passing the Post Office, turn right on a short metalled lane. At the end you'll find a footpath sign in the left hand corner. Follow the field edge path, soon passing Brook Farm over to your right. Keep on past the entrance to the farm, following a surfaced track. In 300m you'll reach a road (Gull Lane).

B: Turn left in Gull Lane and stay on the road for about 400m to a left hand bend. Continue round the bend for 50m, then turn right on a signed path. Cross the field to the stile in the corner, then continue slightly right to join a wide grassy track heading downhill. At the end of the track in about 250m keep straight on along the field edge with the ditch on your right. When you reach the garden of a house in about 800m follow the field edge round to the left to reach a road.

C: At the road go right for about 50m, then left on a signed path. When you reach the corner of the wood, go straight on along the field edge to reach the end of the wood in about 250m. Here you'll reach a T-junction with another track. Turn right on the track to reach a road in about 150m.

D: Turn left on the road, and follow it for about 800m to reach a group of farm buildings on the right hand side.

E: Opposite the farm, turn left through a wooden gate on a signed path. Keep close to the field edge on your left, passing a large reservoir. At the corner of the field in 300m continue on the same line uphill through parkland. After passing the corner of a fence, keep more or less straight on to cross a stile, still staying on the same line to reach a kissing gate onto a road. Turn left on the road for a few steps to reach the T-junction.

F: At the T-junction, turn right to return to the Green in about 800m.

Map 11

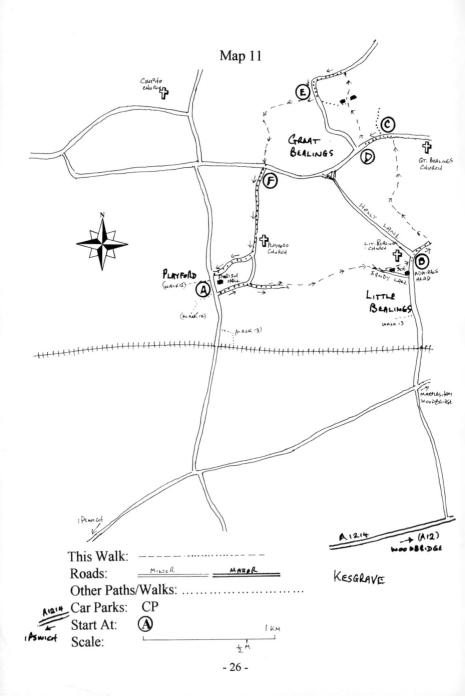

Culphor
Church

E

Great
Bealings

C

D

Gt. Bealings
Church

F

Holly Lane

Playford
Church

Lit. Bealings
Church

B
Admirals
Head

Playford
(Walk 12)

A

Parish
Hall

Spindy Lane

Little
Bealings

(Walk 12)

(Walk 13)

Walk 13

N

Martlesham
Woodbridge

Ipswich

A1214
Woodbridge

Kesgrave

This Walk: ‒ ‒ ‒ ‒ ‒ ‒ ‒ ‒ ‒ ‒
Roads: Minor ━━━━ Major ━━━━
Other Paths/Walks: . . . .
Car Parks: CP
Start At: Ⓐ
Scale:

A1214 Ipswich

(A12)

1 KM

½ M

- 26 -

Walk 11

Distance: 6km (4m) 1 - 1½ hours.
Start Point: Fynn Valley Walk car park, Playford Parish Hall (GR 215477)
Route: Fynn Valley walk, Little Bealings, Great Bealings
Pubs: Admirals Head, Little Bealings
Car Parking: See Start Point

A: Go out onto the road and turn left down Hill Farm Road. In 250m keep right at the fork, following Fynn Valley Walk signs, soon taking a path to the left, again signed Fynn Valley walk. Keep more or less straight ahead for 1km, to reach a road in Little Bealings. Go straight along the road as far as a Primary School then take the path left behind school buildings, reaching a road in 150m. (*The Admirals Head is to the right*).

B: Turn left on the road, and about 150m after passing Holly Lane turn left on a signed path. This soon becomes a field-edge path. Follow the field edge for about 300m to a corner with FP signs then turn right downhill into the neighbouring field. Follow the left hand field edge to emerge in Boot Street, near Great Bealings church.

C: Turn left in Boot Street (Named after an extinct pub called the Boot). Ignore the first signed path on the right, and continue for about another 200m to reach another signed path on the right between houses.

D: Turn right on the path, following a line of wooden power posts to reach a track. *Some locals turn left here as a short cut, bringing them out at the uphill track mentioned below (about 300m). However, this is not an official right of way. The official route is as follows:* Turn right on the track, then follow it round to the left to reach a road. Turn left on the road. Follow the road round to the left in 400m and keep on for 200m to reach an uphill track with a splendid seat carved from a tree stump.

E: Walk up the track, passing the carved seat. Stay on the track for about 1km to reach the Bealings/Tuddenham road.

F: Keep straight on along the narrow road opposite, signed Playford Church. After passing the church in about 600m, follow the road round to the right and stay on it to reach the main road next to the Parish Hall.

Map 12

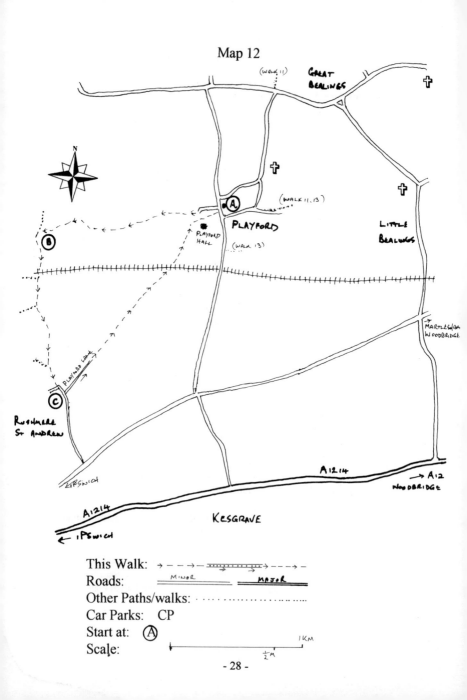

GREAT BEALINGS

(WALK 11)

(WALK 11, 13)

Ⓐ

PLAYFORD

PLAYFORD HALL

(WALK 13)

Ⓑ

LITTLE BEALINGS

MARTLESHAM WOODBRIDGE

PLAYFORD LANE

Ⓒ

RUSHMERE St ANDREW

IPSWICH

A1214

A12 WOODBRIDGE

A1214

KESGRAVE

IPSWICH

This Walk: → – – → – →→→→→ → – – → –
Roads: ———— MINOR   ▬▬▬ MAJOR
Other Paths/walks: ·············
Car Parks: CP
Start at: Ⓐ
Scale: |————————————| 1KM
                ½M

Walk 12

Distance: 4½km (3m) 1 - 1½ hours.
Start Point: Fynn Valley Walk car park, Playford Parish Hall (GR 215477)
Route: Fynn Valley Walk, Rushmere St Andrew, Playford
Pubs: None on route
Car Parking: See Start Point

A: Leave the car park and turn right. In a few steps turn left down the small road by the 'phone box. Follow the lane round to the left in 250m, then almost immediately turn right through a kissing gate into a field. Keep to the right hand field edge. At the end of the field go through another kissing gate. The path meanders through reeds, then, about 75m after passing along the edge of a regimental grove of poplars, you'll reach a 4-way footpath sign.

B: Go on a few steps from the 4-way sign to reach a cross track, then turn left, soon crossing a bridge over the Fynn. Continue up the track on the other side to pass under the railway line. Keep more or less straight on up the lane, ignoring a path to the right almost immediately. In about 200m, again keep straight on, ignoring the bridle path to the right. You'll soon enter a sunken lane. Stay on this to emerge on a corner in Rushmere St Andrew in about 600m.

C: At the corner of the road, go straight on for a few steps, then turn left down Playford Lane. This narrow metalled road becomes a field path with pleasant views in about 500m. Keep straight on to pass over the railway in about 800m. After the bridge, continue on the track on the other side for about 400m. After the bridge, continue on the track on the other side for about 400m. Shortly after passing Playford Hall in trees on your right, turn right to cross an obvious footbridge over a stream. Continue on the path on the other side to reach the road opposite the car park in about 250m.

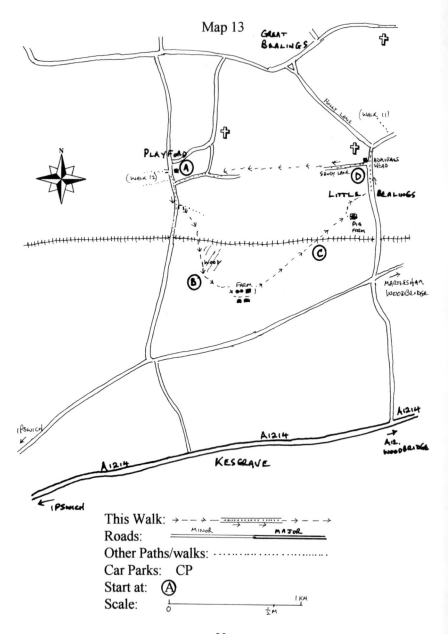

Map 13

GREAT
BEALINGS

(WALK 11)

HOLLY LANE

PLAYFORD

(WALK 12)

Ⓐ

ADMIRALS
HEAD

SANDY LANE

Ⓓ

LITTLE   BEALINGS

PIG
FARM

Ⓒ

WOOD

Ⓑ

FARM

MARTLESHAM
WOODBRIDGE

IPSWICH

A1214

A1214

A12
WOODBRIDGE

A1214

KESGRAVE

A1214

IPSWICH

This Walk:
Roads: MINOR   MAJOR
Other Paths/walks: ··························
Car Parks: CP
Start at: Ⓐ
Scale: 0   1 KM
                              ½ M

- 30 -

Walk 13

Distance: 5km (3m) 1 - 1½ hours.
Start Point: Fynn Valley Walk car park, Playford Village Hall (GR 215477)
Route: Little Bealings, Fynn Valley, Playford
Pubs: Admirals Head, Little Bealings
Car Parking: See above

A: Leave the car park and turn left along the main road, soon crossing the Fynn.   About 150m after the bridge turn left into a signed lane. A few steps along, turn right on the signed path up the field to the stile. Cross the railway with care, then keep on uphill to the right hand corner of the wood. Keep straight along the track by the wood to reach a surfaced farm road at the end.

B: Turn left on the farm road, and stay on it to reach the farm Turn left next to the silos. After passing the house, continue on the signed field edge track. In about 200m cross a lane and go slightly left along the signed path opposite, crossing 2 fields to reach the railway line again.

C: Cross the railway, and keep on towards the pig farm. Just before the farm turn left alongside the buildings and cross the river. Turn right along the track along the river bank to reach the road at Little Bealings. At the road, turn left and walk up as far as Sandy Lane next to the Admiral's Head on the left in about 300m.

D: Turn left up Sandy Lane, and continue along to the end. You are now on the Fynn Valley Walk. Follow this well signed path to emerge on the road in Playford village. When you reach the road, continue straight on to return to the village hall car park.

Map 14

This Walk: → – – → – →⎓⎓⎓⎓⎓⎓→ → – → – →
Roads: ⎓⎓⎓⎓
Other Paths/walks: ....
Car Parks: CP
Start at: **Ⓐ**
Scale:

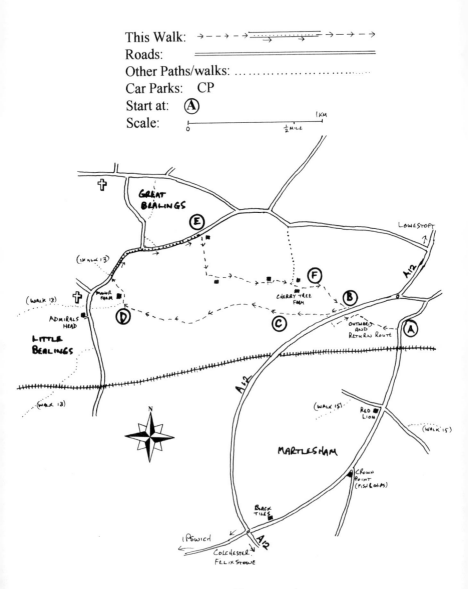

Walk 14

Distance: 5km (3m) 1 - 1½ hours.
Start Point: Martlesham Street (GR 253477)
Route: Fynn Valley, Little Bealings, Great Bealings
Pubs: Admirals Head, Little Bealings (250m off route)
Car Parking: Park on the wide verge at the end of Martlesham street.

A: Take the signed track down through the nursery (Fynn Valley Walk sign). Follow the track along to the A12 then round to the left to reach the tunnel under the road.

B: Pass under the A12 and turn left along the field edge. You'll soon join the River Fynn. Follow the river to cross a plank bridge in 350m, then bear slightly right across the open field to reach a bridge over the Fynn.

C: Follow the well signed path across open fields, then a field edge, then open fields again, towards a large tree at the top of a slope. About 200m after the tree you'll join a track alongside a bank on the left. Follow this as far as a metalled lane in about 150m.

D: Now leaving the Fynn Valley path, turn right to pass a large cream house (Manor Farm), and reach the road in about 350m. *NB. The Admiral's Head is about 250m along the road to the left (i.e. the wrong way) at this point.* Turn right at the road to cross the Fynn road bridge in about 300m. After this, stay on the road for a further 500m to reach a path signposted to Martlesham on the right.

E: Turn right down the driveway, and in 300m follow it round to the left passing a house, keeping alongside the ditch on your left. Cross the stile in the corner and go uphill to reach another stile visible at the top. After crossing the second stile, keep to the field edge, soon passing the front of a cottage. Shortly after the cottage, go into the driveway and continue on to reach Cherry Tree Farm in about 250m.

F: At Cherry Tree Farm, keep more or less straight on, soon heading slightly uphill on a sandy track. In about another 150m, follow the track round to the right towards the A12. When you reach the A12 turn right along the field edge to reach the tunnel, and turn left to reach Martlesham.

Map 15

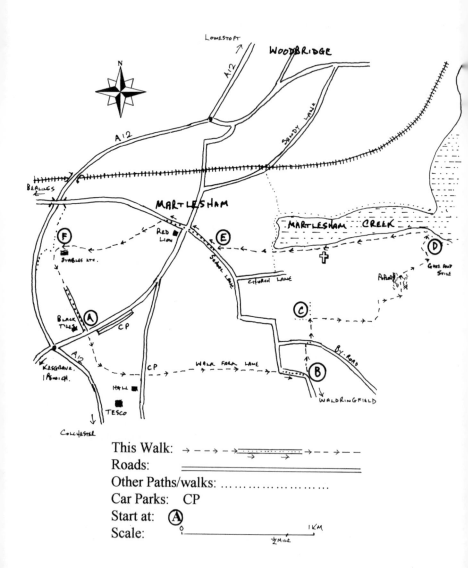

This Walk: → – → – →⟩⟨············⟩ → – → – – –
Roads: ════════════
Other Paths/walks: ....
Car Parks: CP
Start at: Ⓐ
Scale:

Walk 15

Distance: 8½km (5½m) 2 hours approx.
Start Point: Martlesham (GR 244464)
Route: Martlesham Circular Walk
Pubs: Black Tiles, Red Lion
Car Park: Large lay-by in Martlesham on the right after The Black Tiles

A: Take the footpath opposite Black Tiles Lane. When you reach the heath, aim for the red brick buildings (Community Hall) to the left of the Tesco Supermarket. Keep left of the Community Hall to reach a road. Go straight across on the signed path opposite, passing a small car park. Keep more or less straight ahead to emerge on the corner of a road in 1km. Continue along the road for about 200m to where it bends right.

B: Where the road bends right, go left across the field on the signed path. (If in doubt follow the direction of the sign). At the road on the other side, turn right for 50m, then turn left on the track towards Martlesham Hall. In about 100m you'll reach a 4-way footpath sign.

C: Turn right following the field edge to reach a small grove of poplars in about 800m. Turn left for 100m in the poplars, then go right on a track.. Stay on the track for 250m, (ignoring the gap on the right), then cross the stile straight ahead, and turn left along the field edge. After crossing a reedy ditch turn right to reach a stile and plank bridge onto the creek wall.

D: Turn left on the wall. In 500m, at a field edge, turn right, following the line of the creek. In about 400m you'll pass a boat yard. 300m after this you'll reach a cross path. Here go briefly left then right to continue on the same line. In about 700m, you'll reach a road (School Lane).

E: Turn right in School Lane to reach the Red Lion. At the Red Lion, cross over and continue along the road opposite for about 300m to reach a signed footpath on the left. Follow this clear path, mostly along the brook, for about 1km, to reach a 4-way footpath sign close to the A12.

F: Turn left on the cross-path and follow it uphill. Shortly after passing some buildings, the path becomes a metalled road Follow this uphill and onwards to reach the Black Tiles.

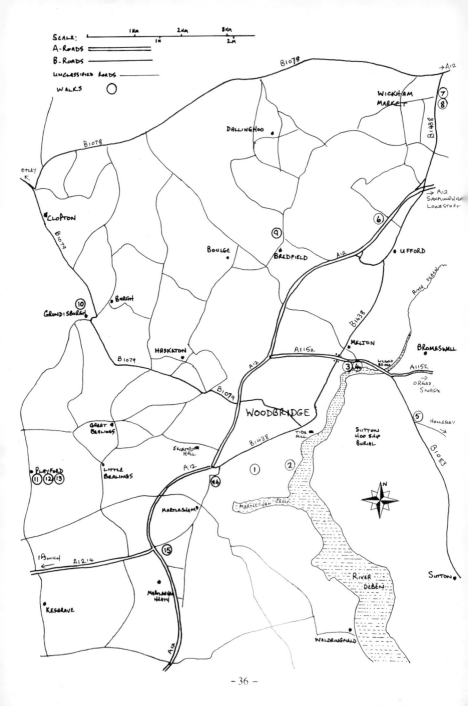

SCALE:
A-ROADS
B-ROADS
UNCLASSIFIED ROADS
WALKS

1KM   2KM   3KM
1M   2M

B1078
→A12
WICKHAM MARKET ⑦ ⑧
B1438
DALLINGHOO
OTLEY
B1078
A12 SAXMUNDHAM LOWESTOFT
CLOPTON
⑨
⑥
B1079
BOULGE   BREDFIELD   UFFORD
River Deben
BURGH
GRUNDISBURGH ⑩
B1438
HASKETON
MELTON   BROMESWELL
A1152
WILFORD BRIDGE
③④
A1152
ORFORD SNAPE
B1079
WOODBRIDGE
⑤ HOLLESLEY
GREAT BEALINGS
B1083
SECKFORD HALL
TIDE MILL
SUTTON HOO SHIP BURIAL
PLAYFORD
⑪⑫⑬
LITTLE BEALINGS
A12
①   ②
⑭
MARTLESHAM CREEK
N
MARTLESHAM
IPSWICH A1214
⑮
RIVER DEBEN
MARTLESHAM HEATH
SUTTON
KESGRAVE
A12
WALDRINGFIELD

- 36 -